# THE YOUNG ADULT'S BLUEPRINT FOR SUCCESS

# THE YOUNG ADULT'S BLUE-PRINT FOR SUCCESS

## Designing Your Life's Playlist and Landing Your First Job Before Graduation

EDITH T. MORICZ, MBA

Published by Advantage, Charleston, South Carolina.
Member of Advantage Media Group.

ADVANTAGE is a registered trademark and the Advantage colophon is a trademark of Advantage Media Group, Inc.

Printed in the United States of America.

ISBN: 978-159932-422-7
LCCN: 2013940276

# IN GRATITUDE

*This book is dedicated to my parents and brother for all of their love, support and belief in my talents and abilities.*

*This book is also dedicated to the memory of Dr. John R. Silber for the impact he has had on my life.*

*Much appreciation and thanks to Entrepreneurial Success Partners for its support of this exciting project, this labor of love.*

*The teenage years are the most valuable years for learning about oneself and preparing for a life of great potential. Many adults don't realize their true potential until their midthirties because they didn't develop the basic foundation for best practices until their midtwenties.*

# Table of Contents

# The Best Years of Your Life

## the Young Adult Years (age 13-17)

*Explore your natural talents.*

*Dig deeper within yourself to expand your knowledge and offer value to your community.*

*Be the best in your area(s) of interest.*

*I'll show you, step by step, how to showcase your talents and spread the word about your knowledge.*

*I'll show you how to be in charge of designing your future and creating your success story.*

*Let's get started . . .*

*"Love what you do and you'll never work a day in your life."*

*Confucius*

# PREFACE

This book will show you what to do during your teenage years to land an exceptional job opportunity well before you graduate from college.

First, the cardinal rule of success—your self-drive, combined with your initiative—defines your life and is responsible for your success. Luck, valuable mentors, funding, and even political connections are not enough to realize your dreams. *You—and you alone—have to want it.* Self-drive and initiative will keep your dreams alive and make what you want worth your time and effort, especially when obstacles are thrown your way.

The key to success in life is how we use our time. A big part of understanding how to use it well is to discover how to gain knowledge at a time when many young adults want to focus only on leisure activities and taking things as they come. The most successful people you will ever meet will tell you that success, in all forms, takes planning, focus, and dedication. This is all well and good, but the secret component to this is making really smart decisions during your younger years, starting when you are 13 or 14 years old. These decisions put you on a trajectory that rewards you richly down the road and enables you to pursue your dream goals.

INTRODUCTION

# Why I Want to Help Young Adults Succeed

I was deeply blessed and immensely fortunate to have been raised in a strict, loving, supportive, and caring family. My brother and I were taught at a young age that hard work, perseverance, and a strong education were the building blocks of success. Highly competitive, we both excelled academically from grade school to high school and into our graduate school years. It was expected that we achieve and achieve notably.

But that's just one side of my story. As a child disabled from birth, I was bullied through most of my years in grade school. Kids can be incredibly cruel (the name calling, the hand gestures, the exclusion from group activities, etc.). Many tears were shed, some publicly, most privately. I know how it is to feel that you don't fit in and that all you want is to be part of a group, to be liked.

No child should have to experience that, but it made me stronger, and it made me work harder to excel academically because then, as I saw it, I would rise above my peers' immaturity and meanness. I would be judged, instead, on my talents and abilities by people whose opinions really mattered. I would be judged on my future potential, as illustrated by my activities as a youngster and young adult.

I also had an incredible family, who never, for a single moment, ever made me feel less than spectacular. But I still had to deal everyday with the cruel kids at school.

I wrote this book to help young adults realize that their ideas are powerful and they are completely in control of their future success. Don't let anyone let you think or, worse, believe otherwise. You are destined to have a successful future *if* you take charge of your young-adult years by implementing my blueprint for success. I would be delighted to hear about your success story. Better still, I would love to interview you as a young entrepreneur in my magazine. Share your success story with me at edith@beyondsuccessonline.com

## WHY I CREATED BEYONDSUCCESSONLINE.COM AND WHY YOU SHOULD CARE

A few of my interests are journalism, mobile marketing, website design, and social entrepreneurism. In 2009, I wanted an effective and fun alternative to business networking. Through trial and error, and spending countless hours browsing Twitter and LinkedIn profiles and learning about their features, I decided that it would be enjoyable and efficient to interview successful business owners via e-mail and share their stories via social media. I focused mainly on business owners who excelled in product design. Social media made it almost effortless to find interesting and talented people. E-mail made it a cinch to contact them. My love of marketing and sales made it an exhilarating challenge to grab their attention and persuade them to give me 15 minutes of their time in return for some publicity. Since 2009, over 150 global entrepreneurs have made my weekly interviews a source of anticipation for my readers and me. I'm fortunate to have received wonderful support and adulation from my peers and business leaders around the globe because of this free resource that I created for start-ups. And to think it began as a fun idea for networking and learning about effectively managing a business. Lesson learned: follow your creative juices, leverage your talents, help others.

BeyondSuccessOnline (BSO) has become my creative outlet for the past several years. It has helped me grow professionally and personally as I have learned about the habits and rituals adopted by sharp, highly motivated, self-disciplined members of our community who poured their money, heart, and soul into pursuing a dream that put them in the driver's seat. I'm deeply impressed by how each of them has carved out their own path to success. Ultimately, we are here on earth to use our talents and add value to our community. Whatever your passion is, maximize it fully and use it to benefit the lives of others.

Hard work, initiative, and a specific focus on enjoyable activities separate the high achievers from those who have merely goals and dreams but don't advance toward them. Action turns goals into reality and the best practices in this handbook will help you live in the reality of your dreams.

### DEFINE YOUR PASSIONS

Focus your energies on areas of high interest, be they artistic talent, intellectual pursuits, charitable causes, athletic abilities—whatever you truly have fun doing and what comes naturally to you. Ask yourself what hobbies bring you the most joy.

You will completely enjoy your future success if your work is tied into an area of natural passion. Perhaps you will find opportunities to combine many passions for important projects that make a difference in your community. As long as you enjoy your activity, it will never feel like work. This will have a significant impact on your career success for whichever industry you choose to pursue.

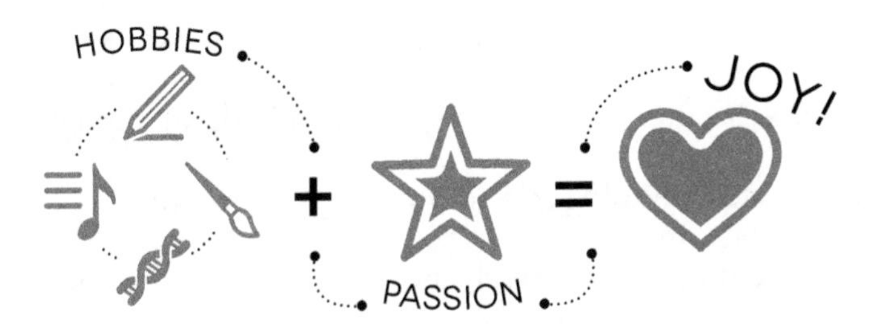


As I previously mentioned, some of my many areas of interest are journalism, web site design, mobile technology, and small business development. I enjoy learning how successful and creative innovators live their

lives and how they ensure that each day is surrounded by creativity and efficiency. Thus, this fueled the creation of my e-zine, BeyondSuccessOnline.com.

In your young-adult years, the sooner you master the best practices of living in excellence,

the sooner you are on your way to living your full potential, unhindered by self-doubt and lack of resources. Living in excellence means embracing the highest standards of performance and doing so with integrity, clarity, and discipline on a daily basis. It means managing your time well (focus on high priority tasks first, one task at a time; multitasking has its place depending on what you are trying to accomplish) and planning your daily activities based on your goals. Achieve two to three specific goals per day following the SMART principle (goals need to be specific, measurable, actionable, realistic and time based). Akin to a school paper you must hand in, you are given the due date and the exact work you need to do. Most importantly, you are capable of doing it.

Living in excellence also identifies the characteristics of accepted industry standards of perfection. These are known as Best Practices. One of the many reasons I created my online magazine, BeyondSuccessOnline.com, is because, at this stage of my career, I wanted to learn about the innovative daily habits of successful entrepreneurs. I derive great personal satisfaction learning how experts in various fields incorporate excellence into their daily lives.

In 2009, I created an online magazine (www.beyondsuccessonline.com) in which I interview some of the best-known, successful entrepreneurs in the world to learn and share their best practices (see Best Practices at the end of the book). My interviews with these accomplished and talented professionals have provided examples of excellence on a daily basis for many years. To be a top performer requires consistency, focus, and a clear plan based on a goal. This plays a large role in distinguishing success from failure and empowering business owners to progress to a profitable future. Joy in your field of interest, a strong desire for continued learning, and enthusiasm in building partnerships are the main ingredients for a stable career, regardless of the industry you choose.

The choices you make as a young adult will lay the foundation for the most promising future you could ever have envisioned. You are about to embark on a journey that will provide you with the essential tools for life-long success. Years from now, you will

look back with pride for what you've accomplished and for the life you've carved out for yourself. Congratulations for making the choice to invest your time and energy in yourself.

The time is right to begin now.

# The Young Adult's Blueprint for Success

## BASIC FINANCIAL SECURITY: THE ROLE OF MONEY

Money certainly provides the means to helping you choose your path of interest, but that's just one piece of it. We will discuss the importance of a personal budget later, but just know that, although money is important to achieving success, there are plenty of other factors equally critical.

The other components of a life well lived are enhanced by financial security and also created by it. Funding allows you to explore your hobbies and certain hobbies draw you into a circle of larger wealth. Thus, wise choices regarding how leisure time is spent play a significant role in exposure to "the good life."

Financial security must be earned for it to be appreciated. Financial security goes hand in hand with true joy in the heart. People who enjoy life bring out the best in others. I have met very few affluent individuals who didn't want to share their lives with a close group of friends. Alternatively, it is true that many professionals choose careers that reward them financially but are not their true passion. My word of caution to you is that, if success requires intense dedication, initiative and persistence to forge ahead when faced with obstacles (and there will be plenty), wouldn't it also be true that passion and enjoyment of your work is a prerequisite to the countless hours focused on doing a great job? Money itself will never be a sole motivating factor.

## ACTIVITIES PURSUED WITH PASSION

When you find an activity that brings you joy, master it and become an expert. Similarly, pursue activities that encourage your abilities. You will experience far greater fulfillment by focusing on sharpening your talent than correcting your flaws. This will also define who you are, so spending many hours perfecting your work will be a pleasure, not a chore.

# The Nine Steps to Success

Our journey through the best practices for achieving excellence in life (and landing your first job before graduation) will focus on nine areas:

1. Smart jobs
2. Brand yourself
3. Building blocks of simple living
4. Mentors
5. Internships
6. Health/wellness
7. Personal development
8. Financial savvy
9. Networking

## 1. SMART JOBS

The organizations you choose to work for will say a lot about your affiliations and strategic plan. Keep in mind that, although you will possibly change career paths at some point or multiple points, make sure you choose organizations that mesh with your values and ones that you can be proud to talk about as you walk through your resume history with prospective employers.

Keep in mind also to expose yourself to big and small organizations. Large corporations offer huge resources in terms of people and training. Take advantage of these opportunities. Small organizations "force" you to learn quickly, trial by fire in many cases. However, you take on multiple responsibilities, which give you significant visibility. I have been able to illustrate more examples of my leadership style while managing volunteers and staff at small organizations. It simply comes with the territory.

Your time spent at jobs matters a lot. Choose wisely and have fun learning.

**A.** Expose yourself to multiple industries by exploring work through internships and part-time jobs. Try retail, financial services, health care, the hospitality industry, banking, and telecommunications, to name a few. Choose three mentors to guide you (three will provide a diversified perspective). Your local community career center and local youth organizations are great resources as well. Contact your parents' high school and college-alumni center for recommendations also.

It's not always about money, so let's get that notion out of the way. Young adults need to hit the pause button on *$$$* and get motivated solely by learning new experiences. Picking up valuable skills and being shown the proper techniques in a professional environment are priceless moments. Many critical learning experiences occur during an unpaid internship. Seize the opportunity or else the next person will—you'll have plenty of time to be greedy later.

Choose jobs that have meaning and purpose, that challenge you, and that you are proud of having. Choose jobs that are demanding and thought-provoking, ones that add value in your daily interaction. Whatever jobs you choose, make them worthy of your time and effort. Give your 110 percent. Focus on making good impressions so that you become the worker everyone wants to see again the next summer or throughout the year. Better still, summer and part-time jobs lead to exciting opportunities when your boss takes you under his or her wing and connects you to his or her network. Your goal is to expand your horizons. This is a valuable way to do it.

**B.** Before you begin high school, or during your summer break in your freshman year, take as

many online classes and webinars as you can. MIT, Harvard, and many other prestigious universities throughout the country now offer free online classes. Check www.edx.org for more information. Choose three topics you have an interest in and three topics (business, law, information technology, psychology, health care, or science) you want to learn more about. Many online courses offer credits that can be applied to collegiate studies. This is a smart and efficient way to learn at your own pace while earning credit toward future college classes.

This is also a smart way to learn how to study. It will be very important for you to figure out what method of studying works best for you. Everyone has different styles and preferences that are most effective. The bottom line is retention. If you learn best re-reading material and reciting it as if you were presenting it without notes to an audience, allow yourself the extra time for this technique.

I was fortunate to have photographic memory. This was very handy when needing to memorize huge amounts of data that were strictly formulaic. However, I required a near silent atmosphere for my study technique to be effective. The plus side is that, fortunately, I was able to focus on information for long hours at a time and I trained myself to constantly (and I do mean constantly) recite in my mind the information I had just read. Also, this only works when your mind is sharp and focused so plenty of sleep was critical. Cramming information never appealed to me and I discourage it, as it is not genuine learning. It's merely "getting by." You will miss out on the true essence of expanding your knowledge if you rely heavily on cramming. Of course, repetition is a key studying technique so, for me, it worked. Again, find out what works best for you because you will need every advantage in absorbing information quickly so that you create efficient and effective study habits.

In the same vein, strengthening your writing skills is essential to your academic and professional success. Your writing style will define you so invest in making sure yours reflects positively your abilities. See www.ehow.com/info_8172566_online-writing-classes.html#page=0.

**C.** Understanding and supporting social philanthropy is essential in terms of community relations.

Broaden your knowledge of social missions, social entrepreneurs, and small-business owners. Learn what goes on behind the scenes in the nonprofit industry. I highly recommend tuning in to Ventureneer.com, created by Geri Stengel to be an excellent resource for nonprofit organizational learning, business development, and management. Her list of speakers and her topics are dynamic and exciting; listening to these discussions from experts around the country will supplement your creative thinking.

## 2. BRAND YOURSELF

How you portray yourself to the community during your young-adult years will make or break the vision you create for your future success. Make a favorable one through your digital footprint. Think of it this way: you want a potential mentor to immediately see your emotional and intellectual maturity. All of your talents will only be viewed as valuable if your first impression is one of readiness to learn and grow as an adult. Focus on ensuring that your pursuit of excellence and higher knowledge is showcased in an impressive way in the years to come.

**A.** Create a blog and post weekly immediately actionable ideas for organizations on improving some aspect of their operations. Reference a specific company site. Keep in mind that cutting costs, increasing revenue, and increasing their customer base are typically what matter most to organizations unless they are in a beta phase and tweaking processes. The assumption here is that your writing skill is highly engaging (remember to focus on how you can help *them*) and thought provoking. If it isn't, work with a creative writing counselor (plenty of career coaches offer this service or look into community colleges for low-cost workshops) to ramp it up. Throughout your academic and professional history, your writing will define you. Make yourself unforgettable and worthy of being shared across the Internet where your future employer can find you later.

Focus on specific industries where you have had direct experience, for example, did you grow up working in the restaurant industry? Does your family own a farm? Do you enjoy the retail industry? What sector(s) have you had direct experience in that led you to ultimately bring in more customers or increase profits? Use your real-life experience to help companies be profitable. Make it easy for them to contact you for further help. You just created your first branding campaign.

**B.** Establish your vanity digital footprint with your branded social-media profiles (Twitter, LinkedIn, Facebook, and Pinterest). The goal is to showcase your skill sets by sharing your ideas and opinions on topics of importance to a target audience. Keep the focus on "I enjoy ____ and here are the three ways that I can help your organization _____(it needs to focus on growth, expansion, profitability)." As you share your life experiences, hobbies and skill sets, you will be connecting with followers who have found commonality with you.

**C.** Contribute articles to magazines and/or blogs that reach your target audience. This will become part of your branding campaign where followers turn into clients with the proper marketing campaign in place.

**D.** Support (volunteer, telemarket, sponsor your own fundraising party with your friends) up to three philanthropic causes that tie in with your life experiences (pets, cancer research/survivors, environmental advocacy, counseling for low-income families, etc.). Give of yourself through causes that are meaningful. The impact of your work will speak for itself and help those less fortunate.

## 3. BUILDING BLOCKS OF SIMPLE LIVING

Only when you appreciate the simplest components of a content existence can you fully appreciate the vast power that your talents have in taking you wherever you want to go. Expand your choices by exposing yourself to the riches of a good life as defined by intelligence and being in control every day of the choices you made.

**A.** Read, react, and enact. One of the greatest gifts of the young adult years is the ability to expand your knowledge. This is a lifelong learning process made exciting based on your level of interest and exposure to the world (travel, languages learned, cultures experienced). Your choices for reading will be unique; pick wisely. I believe firmly in not reinventing the wheel but, rather, learning from the life experiences of people smarter than I am. I then assess how I can incorporate their philosophies and daily activities into my day to improve myself and showcase my skills to the community.

Speaking of showcasing your skills, I was fortunate to connect with Chrissie Lightfoot, Esq. of Leeds, United Kingdom, through LinkedIn. She graciously allowed me to feature her success story in BeyondSuccessOnline's February 23, 2012, issue. I highly recommend her book, *Naked Lawyer*. It speaks of the path of a lawyer who chose to turn the legal profession into an entrepreneurial pursuit in a way that the industry has never experienced before.

What I enjoyed most about it, though, was her journey through her young-adult years, as she had a clear focus of learning for each decade of her life. She had thought it through and spent the years in a massive intellectual and emotional growth to arrive at her successes today. It is inspiring, stimulating, strategic, and witty on numerous levels and will only enhance your drive and enthusiasm for achieving excellence in your life, as you strive to reach your potential and pursue your first job well before college graduation.

**B.** Keep your mind busy and keep your body in motion. Incorporate a wellness/fitness ritual into your weekly regimen (do something different and fun each day to stay motivated). Design it so that it works for you by being enjoyable and habit forming. It should make you feel energized and strong. It should be easily incorporated into your hectic schedule. Most importantly, it needs to be effective. Numbers don't lie, whether it's the bathroom scale, your cholesterol, or blood pressure reading. You alone are responsible for taking care of yourself. You answer to no one but yourself.

**C.** Energy and creative thinking on the run: When I'm on the go, I always carry a bag of about 20 almonds, a kid-sized dark chocolate bar (my way of controlling portion size and sugar content), a pack of spearmint sugar-free gum (an effective mental boost!), and a pocket-sized note pad. These food choices give me instant and smart energy without the unnecessary calories and high fat content. They also prevent me from sabotaging my healthy eating habits by making poor spontaneous choices due to stress or fatigue. The gum and

note pad always keep my creativity flowing and allow me to capture ideas for my magazine, teaching curriculum and mobile marketing, while I'm on the go.

## 4. MENTORS

In addition to building your own knowledge base, I can't emphasize enough how valuable mentors are to your levels of achievement. Among other things, they will be vital to helping you learn about the your skill sets, how people interact, and how different organizations operate—all very useful knowledge to have as a young adult, without having to reinvent the wheel.

Mentors are individuals who help you grow as a person and, as you begin to make career choices, as a professional by providing you with ideas based on their own experiences. As I learned many years ago, every person you meet in your life, particularly in your teenage years, has significant value based on *what* they have experienced in their lives. Regardless of where they are from or the path they have chosen, the perspectives they share with you are unique and meant to help you grow. Therefore, see your interactions as learning experiences. Always ask yourself, "What does this mean to me? How can I better myself based on what I learned today?" Choose your mentors based on their approachability, candor, wit, and humor. In fact, choose a mix of personalities opposite of your own. You will certainly gain very valuable expertise from someone who is radially different than you.  Each will bring strengths to your learning process. Savor the rewarding experience so that you can pass along the experience when you mentor a young adult.

**A.** Pick a few mentors based on age and industry. If you are a freshman in high school, choose a mentor who is a freshman in college, another who has been working professionally for one to three years, and another who has spent 10 years or more in his/her profession. This will give you a great perspective on different industries, career management in terms of age, and ideas for leveraging your talents.

I can't stress enough the importance of mentors to your future success. The sooner you surround yourself with amazing people who are incredibly talented in their own right, the sooner your creative juices will expand and you will see once-in-a-lifetime opportunities come your way.

*SUCCESS* magazine is a source of great ideas, inspiring stories, and insightful tips on being your very best in your daily life, whether personal pursuits or business ventures. I recommend it as part of your monthly reading (www.success.com).

Keep your mind open and gravitate toward people who share your interests. Birds of a feather do flock together, and surrounding yourself with highly intelligent people has spectacular effects. A mentor provides exposure to highly respected members of the community and ideas that propel you to explore stimulating areas of interest. Doors open and whole new worlds wait. It all starts with a person willing and proud to help you launch yourself to a higher level of excellence.

**B.** Choose a mentor who has spent a decade or more in fundraising. In order to be an effective fundraiser, presentation skills, problem solving, multitasking, creative thinking, and IT skills need to be spectacular. It is akin to a small-business owner with a shoestring budget creating demand for services while strategically planning the company's future. This type of mentor, who has seen a lot in terms of leadership styles and which career decisions don't work out so well, can be an invaluable resource.

## 5. INTERNSHIPS

My career in financial services got a head start after an internship at Merrill Lynch during my final semester as an undergraduate at Boston University. It was my most valued work experience ever. Ensure that you learn something every day about the industry by offering your help beyond regular business hours (stay past 5 p.m. and show your eagerness to be a team player). It will make a huge difference to you and the organization.

**A.** An internship (likely unpaid) with a nonprofit organization will be an exceptional experience for you. The level of resourcefulness required with an unimaginably low budget will amaze you. In fact, it's this resourcefulness combined with creativity that will enable a nonprofit to excel or crash.

**B.** Go above and beyond your responsibilities in every job. Do it to gain added understanding of your industry but more, to learn from your team members. Some of the most senior level jobs were obtained from working in an internship and being "discovered" by the right individual who recognizes your talent. An internship is a hidden gem in terms of exposure, learning, and connecting with people. If you can intern throughout your high-school year and in your early college years, seize the opportunity.

**C.** Throughout your high-school years, choose four different nonprofit organizations and volunteer your time at one each year. The operations and program management positions alone will shed light on the world of philanthropy and will add an extra layer to your ability to work with people from diverse backgrounds. Watch them solve problems as a team.

See how they handle conflicts and celebrate victories. Watch how they impact the community through their daily activities. The spirit at most nonprofits is infectious, so don't be surprised if it motivates you to pick a special cause and perhaps start your own charitable mission midway through high school.

## 6. HEALTH/WELLNESS

Put first priority on your daily health maintenance. It'll be the best decision you make every day. Do everything you can to preserve it. It'll pay you back in years to come.

**A.** Vitamin supplements, in conjunction with smart meal choices and a disciplined exercise regimen, are essential in providing you with lasting energy and vitality as you take on your daily activities. A strong, healthy heart, muscles that are kept active, and a sharp mind—all are necessary to allow you the ability to focus clearly on your agenda. To be at your best each day and to keep your body at its prime, I recommend the following supplements for nurturing all of your major muscles, your skin, and your heart, and for replenishing cells from daily cellular breakdown: A multivitamin, Vitamin A, C, D, B (B1, B2, B3, B5, B6, B7, B9, B12), vitamin D3, Vitamin E, and K. See www.livestrong.com for suggested daily requirements. With your active lifestyle, your meals will not adequately give you the daily boost you require to stay healthy and keep a strong immune system.

**B.** Keep your meal choices simple: organize part of your weekend to plan for a week's worth of healthy snack or meal options at your fingertips. If you don't buy it, you won't be tempted by it. Berries, nuts, fat-free or low-fat dairy, grains (wheat bread, steamed rice), lean protein (white chicken, fish, and eggs), and steamed vegetables are all healthy. Squash sweet cravings through bite-sized dark chocolate, apples, bananas, grapes, and berries. Minimize caffeine intake (a cup in the morning is adequate). Choose extra sleep over caffeinated beverages.

**C.** Keep your energy level optimized by consuming no more than six grams of sugar at each meal. Like salt, using sugar sparingly is fine. Just be mindful of your consumption. Spare yourself the prospect of adult diabetes by minimizing your intake. Sugar simply turns to fat cells, for which you have no use. Log your meals for a week and be very mindful of how much sugar you consume.

**D.** Start your day and end your day with a glass of water. Hydration is critical for your body to operate efficiently. Jumpstart your morning with a glass of water and a slice

of lemon. The lemon's vitamin C will give you part of your RDA. Do the same two hours before bedtime for proper cleansing. It's a great little habit to incorporate in your daily routine.

**E.** Minimize your alcohol and caffeine consumption.

I believe in giving my body every advantage I can, so I never had any interest in alcohol or in coffee. For a healthier future, minimize your alcohol and caffeine consumption.

You've probably heard this advice a million times, but indulge me. When I was in high school, there was never a big emphasis on caffeine. As in all schools, alcohol was shunned. But at my school, so was caffeine. Truth be told, I never had coffee until well past my college years (I preferred extra sleep). So I truly do not understand this obsession with caffeine during the high-school years. Coffee only became a fad after Starbucks started popping up on every street corner and carrying your coffee paper cup made you a member of the "cool" group. I hate to rain on your frothy party, but as you get older and realize that your caffeine addiction will have a significant effect on your cardio health and blood pressure, you'll rethink all those years you cavalierly paid $4 for a cup of java.

ONLY ONE CUP PER DAY!

My advice? Stick to one cup in the morning and, after 3 p.m., hydrate with water and nonsugary juices. Ladies, make it part of your beauty regimen. Your skin will thank you. Having avoided caffeine for most of my adult years, I prefer herbal tea. I have been fortunate to have had clear, healthy-looking skin. And by the way, it makes a difference to have a youthful face, rather than skin that screams "I haven't slept in years." And, unless you want to invest in expensive skin care treatments, reversing the damage is almost impossible.

I highly recommend that you to seek the advice of a certified nutritionist. She or he will ask you to log your food intake for a week. It is illuminating to examine your diet log and learn in your younger years which foods are healthy and which ones aren't. It's never too late to adjust your nutritional habits, but certainly the sooner you start, you sooner you will reap the benefits of clean eating.

**F.** Meditate/contemplate/design: Set aside 30 minutes during each day (based on your body chemistry) to capture ideas that are "floating" in your head and to jot down goals for the week (create blog content, make five new contacts, sign up for two webinars, and so on).

**G.** Body rhythm: Be very mindful of your best hours in the day to be productive and to brainstorm. I'm an early riser so I do all my creative thinking and writing between 6:30 a.m. and 10:30 a.m. However, my body rhythm for exercise is late morning or 2 p.m. to 3 p.m., so I structure my exercise routine around that timetable. Work with your body's flow, not against it. The results speak for themselves.

**H.** The body is meant to be in motion. We all know the damaging effects of a sedentary lifestyle, so

find activities that you enjoy and keep you active. Make fitness a regular part of your day. Think of it as your daily maintenance. Choose activities that energize you and are enjoyable. They will make daily movement feel fun and you'll want to do it longer at each workout session. I highly recommend consulting a personal fitness trainer on what would be the optimal exercise routine you should engage in, since everyone's needs are unique and personal one-on-one consultation on exercise is by far more effective than doing it on your own. I worked with a personal trainer for several years because I wanted to adjust my exercise routine to further challenge my body. I was well past my young-

adult years, but the difference that this investment made in my life is incalculable. I often ponder how effective it would have been had I started in my early adult years.

**I.** Make sure to get at least seven to eight hours of sleep if you want to be able to function at your level best. Sleep is how your brain recharges and reawakens its creative energy. Depriving yourself of adequate sleep is one of the biggest physical disservices you can do to yourself. Many medical

symptoms and ailments are caused by lack of sleep (www.SleepTracks.org). Over the years, the sleep you will have missed adds up and it will curtail your future plans of success while posing a serious health hazard. Why not be good to your body? It's the only one you have.

## 7. PERSONAL DEVELOPMENT

Personal development, besides good health/wellness, is the most important for you to understand. Nothing is more pivotal to the achievement of your dreams. Yet the window of opportunity to truly take advantage of this growth is short, so please don't squander it. Make investing in your personal development your number-one priority. I assure you it'll make all the difference in the world.

**A.** Speaking enables you to be a master of your voice, your presence, and your message (own the room with confidence and poise). I highly recommend Susan Berkley's www.GreatVoice.com as a resource. Everyone can improve vocal presentation. You'll hear an immediate difference in your voice presentation once you follow Ms. Berkley's suggestions.

**B.** Watch the video presentations of leaders you admire. Pay attention to their style and message. This will be a very powerful tool for you as you explore diverse topics. You'll quickly discover that much of your success in your future will be determined by your comfort level speaking to crowds and your level of engagement during your presentation. When you feel passionate about your topic and thoroughly confident about yourself, it's very obvious and very attractive to your audience. As you do with your favorite sport, practice until you feel confident enough to give ad hoc presentations on topics meaningful to you.

Videotape your presentations and forward them to your mentors. Request honest feedback. You will have such a leg-up on your peers if you do this in your freshman/sophomore high school years. The most successful entrepreneurs I interviewed over the past five years all shared the common trait of enjoying performing and the thrill of 'theatrics." Being comfortable with watching yourself on videotape is a significant accomplishment. Imagine the advanced skills you'll be improving once your speaking style has been perfected in your early high-schools years. It puts you in a whole different league of accomplishments when senior professionals *struggle* to be heard. Remember that being a great speaker is more about presentation and confidence than aptitude. Not all brilliant people speak eloquently, but all eloquent speakers are brilliant (hint: it's because that is how they make their audience feel). Those who have aced presentations since school and focus highly on their ability to connect with people are those who attract success.

Connecting becomes influencing becomes persuading. With few exceptions, your career will be based on your ability to draw people close to you, to pay attention to your thoughts, and to be influenced by what you represent (service, product, or philosophy). This is a big reason why great sales professionals experience enormous success in their industry: they are stellar presenters. Be comfortable giving presentations on the fly.

**C.** Negotiating: The secret to negotiating is having information (the more, the better) when stating your case. Never was it truer that knowledge is power than during negotiations. The best book I've ever read on negotiating is *Never Lose Again* by Steve Babitsky and James Mangriviti Jr. It spells out, situation by situation, what information is most necessary and how to leverage it to win negotiations. It's all in the power of what you ask and what information you receive. Listening closely and carefully are the keys to knowing your opponent's weakness.

**D.** Conflict management/people skills are essential for life and work. Master them and you will achieve much success in your future. Listen to all sides of the argument and aim first and foremost for resolution. It takes little effort to get bogged down with politics and "he said/she said." Instead, save your focus and your time for crafting solutions that solve problems. It'll enable you to better handle any kind of audience and will give you a reputation for problem resolution skills, which are critical for success in all professions.

**E.** On a monthly basis, read a self-motivation/business management book (Dan Kennedy, Peter Drucker, and Tony Robbins are good choices) and also the bio or memoir of a business or community leader you admire.

One of the most critical pieces (and best uses) of your young-adult years is learning about diverse topics such as the liberal arts, business, science, and information technology. Being well versed in a wide gamut of topics will provide a strong foundation for determining your skills and talents. It will lead you closer to your passions in life and help you discover your true calling.

Broadening your knowledge will enable you to be more effective in many circles. In all industries, impressions are huge. As you determine what you really enjoy doing, the more exposed you are to industry experts, the more well rounded your ideas will be. This is critical because you will want to approach people with nonpolitical philosophies that take both sides of an argument into account. Once you are familiar with the stances of a given field's experts, you will be respected for your affiliations.

As you get older, personal and work-related responsibilities will demand your time. Self-development reading will feel like a luxury that you need to cram in to feel fulfilled. Enjoy all of the self-development reading (books by Stephen Covey, James Collins, Maria Bartiromo, Carl Jung, Deepak Chopra, Jillian Michaels, Dan Ramsey, Tony Robbins, Bill Gates, Jack Welch, Donald Trump, Ray Kurzweil, Malcolm Gladwell, and Seth Godin to name a few) you can as early in your teenage/young-adult years as you can; you'll be grateful when you reflect on your achievements as an adult.

**F.** Learn to respond well to changes and how to use them to your advantage (your career will depend on it). This will prove to be your biggest asset throughout your life. The key is to quickly accept the fact that change can be very good and will teach you enormous resilience. Having had multiple experiences with resiliency throughout my life, I can say that it has kept my life thoroughly exhilarating and challenging, but, at the core, it has given me a deep sense of confidence, knowing that I can handle any situation that arises.

I transferred (as a dormitory resident) in my second year of college from a women-only liberal arts college with a total population of 600 to (as a commuting student) one of the largest independent universities in the country with an alumni population of 39,000 students. I chose a career in financial services (sales) for 11 years after I obtained my bachelor of science degree and switched to fundraising in the nonprofit sector for the next nine years of my career. The industry went through many changes, of which many were directly a result of economic weakness and the increased demands for community, mission-based services. For sheer fun and the enjoyment of using my self-taught social-media-marketing skills along with my love of journalism, I created BeyondSuccessOnline.com. I have been sharing my findings on best practices in business development (and managing a balanced life) with small-business owners everywhere. Mobile technology has enabled me to efficiently help others while growing my PR base. Resiliency enables and empowers you: do not fear the unknown but, rather, embrace it inquisitively for how it can strengthen your talents. From that vantage point, you will feel in control and make decisions that propel you toward personal development. Ultimately, this is the one building block of success that will impact your ability to navigate your path when various opportunities come your way.

**G.** Priority management—The activities that help you develop yourself (a direct benefit for you) and those that help others (your efforts directly impacting someone else). Finishing up your essay for your French class takes priority over volunteering to help your local church's bake sale. Both are important to you, but the former has a direct effect on your class grade. The latter is an optional activity. You need to put 100% effort into your essay but that likely won't happen if you spend most of your weekend volunteering and getting together with friends. Never put your academic work second to your extra curricular activities. If your grades are average or shoddy, your efforts need to go more towards improving them than to showcasing your interest in philanthropic efforts.

Be very strict about how you compartmentalize your time. I post my social media updates between 5:30 a.m. and 6:30 a.m. because I receive fast responses at that time. Most busy people use the early morning to manage their e-mails. This early morning ritual also exhibits a future management style. It illustrates both efficiency in handling important communications and outreach before the days gets hectic. Hence, use your morning hours wisely when you need to contact people. Social media updates can be addictive due to the back and forth communications but keep in mind that the interactions you need to focus on will yield more than just updates in your inbox. They will be valuable opportunities from people who can help you achieve your full potential. This is what the young adult years are all about.

Whatever task you are assigned, be it schoolwork, an after-school project, or a part-time job, learn as much as you can about it. Your added knowledge will give value to your task immediately and will bring more opportunities your way. Imagine the accumulation of knowledge during your first year of high school if you researched unfamiliar topics. You'll have a significant knowledge base accumulated, which will make you even more valuable to future employers.

**H.** The Rolodex: A friend of mine from grad school told me how he started attending workshops and seminars (with all age groups invited) while in high school. Since freshman year, he started collecting business cards and contact information of fellow attendees and started his first business/social

Rolodex. By the time he was a high-school senior, he had several Rolodexes. Incidentally, he was one of the best connectors I had ever met, low key, easy to approach, and very likeable. He chose a career in financial analysis and, relative to the industry-wide changes I experienced, his career had more stability. His Rolodex idea stuck with me. Don't wait until your first official job to start one.

## 8. FINANCIAL SAVVY

Be smart about how you spend your hard-earned money. Learn about investing your funds and taking some risks initially. Set aside 10 percent of your earnings every month and invest in a high-growth opportunity. Feel the uncertainty. Enjoy the opportunity. It's an exciting experience every young adult should feel. For your own protection, always seek the guidance of a financial advisor to learn about what investments are best suited for your needs and goals.

**A.** As soon as you receive your first paycheck, open your retirement account. The sooner you start depositing money into this account, the better it will be in terms of compounding for performance returns. In this case, time is on your side, so please take advantage of it. Even if you deposit only $2,000 a year at age 14 (versus the full $5000 allowed by law) into your retirement account, the benefits of having an IRA account during your high-school years are significant.

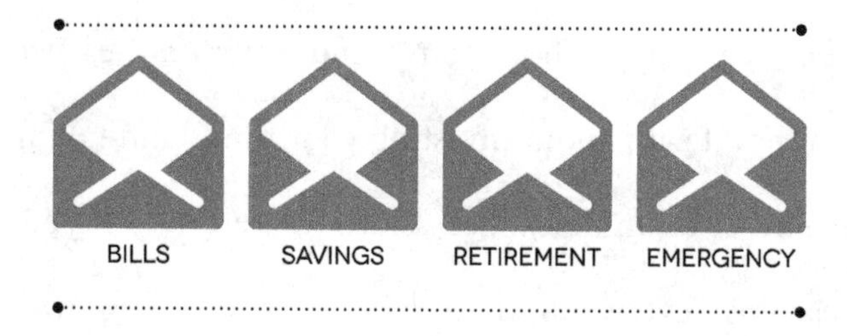


**B.** Cash envelope system: Learn to pay daily expenses with cash and not use credit unless it's either an emergency or a significant expense. Pay off the credit card in full each month or in no more than two months. The cash system is great because it removes the temptation of plastic and makes you more responsible with money management based on your needs and wants. Instant gratification (spontaneous purchases) becomes less important when you consider that you could instead be saving for a secure financial future.

**C.** My 30-30-30-10 percent personal budget rule: First, set aside funds for your long-term future (retirement: 30 percent), and then for your savings account (30 percent), followed by your current expenses (30 percent), with charitable giving at 10 percent. Implement this system and stick to it throughout your career; your financial future will sparkle.

## 9. NETWORKING

"It's who you know that matters in life; less so, what you know." Just make sure you are connecting with people who can teach you and advise you on how to pursue your interests. Spending significant time with people who are not helping you grow is part of the reason why I believe that many young adults are not on the path to success. It all boils down to the company you keep. Friends have a time and place in a young adult's life, but the focus needs to be on adding value to your future goals and ambitions. Enjoying your friends' company is nice, but it will not address your higher intellectual and emotional needs or provide the growth opportunity necessary to expand your knowledge base. Be around people who are smarter than you. Cherish their brilliance and levels of experience. Spend time with different age groups, especially senior citizens who offer great advice and perspectives.

**A.** What can I do for you? Incorporate servicing others into your high-school years. Make it part of how you add value to your community. The contacts you'll make, the projects you help organize, and the experiences you'll have will be priceless. The more you expand your knowledge, people, and experience base, the more you equip yourself for a promising future. President Kennedy said it best: "Ask not what your country can do for you; ask what you can do for your country."

**B.** Get involved in community outreach: speak with two to three community leaders weekly. Find them through your local business journal and community newspaper. Your goal is to introduce yourself and make them aware of who you are and how you can be a valuable resource to them. Start with a letter of introduction and then a phone call, followed by a face-to-face meeting (or Skype if their schedule is frantic).

**C.** Review the websites of local organizations in your community and make recommendations of how you can help them improve their work: Cut costs? Reach more customers? Try an innovative idea and increase profits? Create a custom letterhead using your own design and send them an introductory letter about how you help local companies with your talent. Make a few suggestions based on what you see on the site and say that you will phone their office in a week to share your ideas for increasing their profit. After a phone call/Skype, see if you can arrange a brief meeting to further introduce yourself. The personal touch always cements in the mind of the leader your dedication and desire to do good with your talent, and it offers a glimpse of your problem-solving skills.

# Final Thoughts

I feel privileged to look back upon my most formative years of growth and discovery and share with you the experiences that led me to where I am today. My success today was largely dependent on the structure, focus, and exposure that my parents instilled in my life as a youngster. To have clarity and a vision as a young adult is a significant gift. To enable it to guide you toward a path of success as a person is to live your life to its full potential. To land a challenging and exciting job opportunity based on the talent and skills that you've perfected in your younger years is your well-deserved reward for your pursuit of excellence.

I hope you believe throughout your adult years that your potential is unlimited as long as you stay creative, be true to your heart, and pursue ideas that are meaningful to you. Be guided by the fact that anything is possible as long as you believe in yourself and you feel passionate about a cause. I wish you all of the greatest success in your endeavors. May you create an incredible future for yourself with good health to enjoy it.

# Best Practices

OF SOME OF THE WORLD'S MOST SUCCESSFUL ENTREPRENEURS, AS SHARED WITH ME VIA BEYONDSUCCESSONLINE.COM.

Thoughts on entrepreneurship and/or time management:

1. Bill Attinger

   Founder & CEO of ActSeed Corporation, USA

   www.actseed.com

   *"Vision without execution is nothing. Stop talking, start doing. Embrace imbalance. Don't fight the undertow; surf on top of the wave."*

2. Charles Zeiders

   PhD, Clinical Psychologist, USA

   www.drzeiders.com

   > *"I maintain deep friendships…I always schedule something to look forward to."*

3. Gerald Chertavian

   CEO & Founder of Year Up, USA

   www.yearup.org

   > *"Reputations are earned very slowly and lost very quickly. Learn on someone else's dime before you risk your own."*

4. Elvira Grau

   CEO & Founder of SpaceOdysseyUSA, USA

   www.spaceodysseyusa.com

   > *"Just stick to it (starting a career)—when people jump around too much, they never accomplish anything"*

5. Jay Calderin

   Founder & Executive Director of Boston Fashion Week, USA

   www.bostonfashionweek.com

   ***"Figuring out what is really important in your life is key and it changes at different times in your life. Allow yourself permission to indulge in the things in your life that recharge your spirit."***

6. Jennifer Walsh

   CEO of Behind the Brand Media, USA

   www.behindthebrandmedia.com

   ***"Don't be afraid to take a risk. I've had my fair share of failures along the way but have been able to learn and pick myself up to keep going."***

7. Jennifer Hyman & Jenny Fleiss

   Co-Founders of Rent the Runway, USA

   www.renttherunway.com

   ***"Starting a business is a series of iterative tests. Each test eliminates some of the risks of starting a business."***

8. Lewis Howes

   Founder of Sports Executives Association, USA

   www.lewishowes.com

   ***"Hustle and be passionate; the rest you'll learn along the way."***

9. Polina Raygorodskaya

   Founder & President of Polina Fashion LLC, USA

   www.polinafashion.com

   ***"Go for it. There is never going to be a perfect time. Take calculated risks but don't be blind to what can come. Steer clear of analysis paralysis (over analysis without moving forward)."***

10. Dr. Ruchi Dass

    CEO HealthCursor Consulting Group, India

    www.healthcursor.com

    *"My mantra for time management is PPP- 'Prioritize + Plan = Perfect.' You need to decide how much time you need to allocate to people around you in both corporate and personal spheres of life."*

11. Scott Morrison

    Founder of 3x1 Denim, USA

    twitter.com/3x1

    *"Build your concept/vision/brand around a story (point of view). You need to have one and it needs to be unique if you are going to be successful, no matter what business you are in. Make it a priority to find something you love to do, and try to find a way to make a living doing it."*

12. Vanya Osmanlieva

    Founder of Virtual Assistants, Bulgaria

    virtualassistants.bg

    ***"Never give up! Just when you think that the situation cannot get worse, then something incredible—a miracle—happens and you just succeed! In fact, most people give up a step before they achieve a success. Hard work and loyal attitude are the basis for a grand success!"***

Printed in the USA
CPSIA information can be obtained
at www.ICGtesting.com
JSHW012043140824
68134JS00033B/3238